Wise Courtship

Before Relationship & Marriage Guide

Toni Henderson-Mayers

Word Therapy Publishing, LLC
PO Box 939
Hope Mills, NC 28348
www.WordTherapyPublishing.com

©2016 Toni Henderson-Mayers. All rights reserved.

No part of this book may be reproduced, stored in a retrieval system, or transmitted by any means without the written permission of the author.

Published by Word Therapy Publishing, LLC 2/27/2016

ISBN: 0-9755163-0-2

Library of Congress Control Number: 2016933639

Any people depicted in stock imagery provided by Thinkstock are models, and such images are being used for illustrative purposes only. All other photos were printed with permission from the owner or are public domain.

Because of the dynamic nature of the Internet, any web addresses or links contained in this book may have changed since publication and may no longer be valid. The views expressed in this work are solely those of the author and do not necessarily reflect the views of the publisher, and the publisher hereby disclaims any responsibility for them.

Cover Design: Toni Henderson-Mayers

Dedication

I dedicate this book to my husband. Getting to know you has been fun, interesting and exciting. To my mom and dad who taught me to pray for a good spouse and to GOD for supplying one.

Acknowledgements

I would like to thank the following people for their support of me. These people have been encouragers and/or mentors in my life. To my husband Brian for his endless support and love; my mom, Alma J. Henderson who sets the bar high for me as to what a Christian woman should be; my dad, the Rev. Dr. Steve C. Henderson, Jr. who is with The Lord now and has shown an incredible love for the church and God that I now possess; my siblings and extended family. Special thanks to my nieces April Cox and Anita Evans for reading portions of the book and giving their opinions. I love you guys! To the Arts High Family in general especially the class of 1984, the talent that comes from my alma mater is incredible. 1984 we have been friends for a long time and I love you. To Dr. Reginald Wells our Pastor and great friend, both Brian and I admire your tenacity and your work ethic which has been an inspiration. I appreciate your encouragement and support. Dr. Lorine C. McLeod for encouragement and cheering me on and showing love in my efforts to do right even when others didn't or made life hard for me. Dr. Sharon Cooper-Brooks for being an outstanding mentor who helped me to see further and higher. You are incredible.

To God, I couldn't have done this without you. I've done what you've asked. It's in your hands. (We are now publishing the 2nd edition and have worldwide distribution and audience.)

Thank you.

What people are saying about Wise Courtship

This is a well thought out work that provides important spiritual guidance for couples to move towards marital success in a secular world of frequent marriage dissolutions and painful impact on children. This author is truly on point. Read it now!

-Sharon W. Cooper, MD FAAP
Developmental and Forensic Pediatrician
University of North Carolina at Chapel Hill
School of Medicine

For more testimonials, please go to the back of the book.

Foreword

By Mrs. Cora Jakes-Coleman

Marriage is a mountain some of us choose to climb, and some of us choose to wait. As always before you plan to climb a mountain there are quite a few things you must do before you take your first step. You must make sure you have nourishment for each hurdle and each stop. You must have protection for every slip or even fall. You must have communication with your team, and a way to communicate if you need help.

You must have the necessary tools to get to the goal you have set. Before you even pick a mountain you study it you learn the mountain, and then you prepare to climb it. I have only been married for a year and a half, and I can speak from personal experience when I say climbing this mountain is not easy. I have cried, laughed, smiled, cried some more, and fallen a few times.

There are many things that can prepare you for marriage; communicating with your partner, learning your partner, and pre-marital counseling. I would say pre-marital counseling helped my husband and I out the most. You never know what will happen in the midst of the marriage.

I tell my engaged friends everything you dislike about your mate is emphasized and there is no where you can go. Marriage is a rewarding experience but it takes a lot of work. The best thing you can do when you go before this mountain or a job as well, is to be completely prepared and have the tools you need to conquer the day. That is what pre-marital counseling does for you it gives you the tools necessary to take on the mountains and trials of life.

After I got married my husband and I went through in-vitro fertilization. It was one of the hardest things we went through when we found out the treatment did not work. It shook me and him at our core. I was broken, and confused. Premarital counseling gave us the tools we needed to face our deepest darkest moments and give them light. It taught us not to blame or judge each other but to fight together with love and compassion.

Marriage is not all cake and ice cream it truly is a mountain. There will be hurdles there will be hard times. You may get scrapes, cuts, bruises, and you will get tired, just like any test or trial we go through. When you get to the top of the mountain after all the hurdles, and all the scrapes - when you get to the top and you get to look back on all you went through to get there, it makes every hurdle, pain, and fall worth it. The trick is *how* you take on the next mountain, because there will *always* be a mountain to climb. My best remedy for constant mountain climbing is to work on it together.

Cora Coleman is a mother, daughter, sister and wife. She works as Nursery Coordinator of the Potter's House of Dallas. Cora was born in West Virginia, but raised in Texas by parents Bishop and First Lady Jakes along with four other siblings. Mother of a wonderful daughter along with her husband whom she absolutely adores, she treasures the ability to encourage people through her stories and life experience. She desires to write children books, and open her own childcare facility. Currently Cora writes in a blog very close to her heart www.fertilityfaith.com about her journey of infertility, foster care, and adoption. Cora loves helping people and nurturing the generation of today and tomorrow.

Reading this book will help you decide who is best suited to help you climb mountains, as Cora puts it and not create new ones.

Table of contents

1. Are you sure you are ready to walk down the aisle?
2. Do you know this person?
3. What you see *is* what you get.
4. Let the buyer beware!
5. No refunds, no returns.
6. A wedding gift for you.
7. More love gifts

It was because your hearts were hard that Moses wrote you this law," Jesus replied.

Mark 10:5

Are you sure you are ready to walk down the aisle?

An Introduction

A great writer

I have a confession to make. I am not a great writer, great theologian or even a great thinker. I do serve a great God who has laid a great and heavy burden on my heart to share and remind His people of principles He left many years ago in His Word. The bible says, *"My people are destroyed from lack of knowledge."* **(Hosea 4:6, NIV)** If the knowledge of God is not studied, practiced and passed down from generation to generation, we will soon perish. With every generation, generally speaking, something is lost and we begin to see evidence of a breakdown, especially in our families and relationships. Please allow me to share a little of what I believe God has given to me.

Just trying to help

This book is intended to be a helpful guide. I do not have all the answers, but God does. It is my prayer that something in this book will encourage you to read and study God's Word further for the answers in life you seek. Ask God for direction and to reveal to you what He wants to happen in your life. If you do, you'll never go wrong.

Society looks to many people as experts. What's amazing is we seek advice from those who really are not successful in the area they are giving advice. Counselors who have many troubles themselves, parent advice from a parent with unruly children, relationship advice from those with many broken relationships is commonplace. Although no one is perfect, there are some who have had success in a certain area. We can learn a lot from those who have made mistakes, but we can only learn what went wrong and what not to do. Perfection is far from all of us; however, there are some areas in all of our lives, where God has given us strength and success. It is our duty and privilege to share those experiences with others. A person who is successful in an area can teach you how to do it too. What would this world look like if we all helped to strengthen those areas where others were weak? What would you look like if someone helped you?

I pray this book will empower you, strengthen you and encourage you and most importantly, teach you how to identify and cherish, love.

Are you ready?

One of the toughest questions you will need to ask yourself is, "Am I ready to be married?" On the surface, the answer may seem obvious since there may be an inner urge to unite with someone else. However, when one ponders the question deeply other questions may also arise. For instance, "What makes me so sure I am ready to marry?", "What do I have to offer my potential partner?", "What flaws do I possess that would make it difficult for someone else to unite with me?", "Am I willing to make amends to be marriage ready?" This is by no means a thorough list of all that one may need to ask themselves years before walking down the aisle. The point is however that questions need to be asked of oneself as soon as the thought of marriage enters one's mind. Actually, I believe these questions should be considered even before a courtship begins.

The task of asking oneself thought provoking questions and being blatantly honest may not be easy but has to be done. You will need to be honest with yourself, answer the questions and be brave enough to follow through on what needs to be remedied. Self-reflection and improvement is a task for the courageous. It may be a lot of work upfront, but is extremely fruitful when completed. It will save you a lot of future heartache. Include family and friends in this exercise. Anyone who knows you well and loves you and wants the best for you can be an asset. With the right combination of God, self, family and friends you will be able to see a realistic picture of yourself and your readiness for lifetime relationship with another person.

Is your partner ready?

This book comes from the premise that you are ready for commitment, but is your partner? Within the following chapters there is information to help you assess your partner's readiness. We cannot read anyone's mind, but we have to do our homework to determine how ready our partner may or may not be. Your happiness is on the line. The work is worth it.

In addition, let me say that we cannot force someone to be ready or make them ready for us. Each of us is ready at different times in our lives if at all. If you force a person to be ready and they are not, the relationship might fail.

Is your environment ready?

At first glance you may be thinking what on earth does the environment has to do with my relationship. I'm referring to the environment in which we live, mingle, work, worship and the like. Do you have drama in your life? What dynamics are present in your family? Are your friends busy bodies, tend to mettle? What will your church's reaction be? How does your church handle change? Do you have a plan for any of the questions asked? Will your partner have an adverse reaction to any of these environmental conditions? Have you asked them? Do you care? Don't assume that your partner will just fall in line. You may be used to your crack head sister barging into your home asking for money, disturbing peace and causing trouble, but your potential spouse may not like the idea.

It is amazing what we grow use to in our lives; even dysfunctions. Don't expect your potential spouse will want to get use to your dysfunctional or functional life.

Did God tell you?

Did you ask God what He thought? In order to find out what God thinks, you need to ask him. You ask God His thoughts through prayer, meditating on scripture and listening for His response. God will answer audibly, through scripture, a sermon, friends, guidance or in a variety of ways. No matter how you receive a response, make sure you receive one and you are totally clear on His direction.

Many people skip this crucial step, but this is a huge mistake. If you are not sure God told you to marry this person, DON'T. The marriage will fail.

Everyone may not consider marriage as an option, but even if you are in a relationship that you may not be taking seriously, please consider these helpful hints.

"But at the beginning of the creation, God 'made them male and female.'

Mark 10:6

Do you know this person?

Ask questions. I can't provide a simpler and more effective form of guidance. Get to know this person you plan on spending the rest of your life with. And it will be the *rest of your life*! The marriage will not be over because you become tired or bored or aggravated or even frustrated. Well at least it shouldn't be.

I'm sure you are well aware of the terrible state marriage is in these days. Over half of all marriages end in divorce. Over 80% of failed marriages, failed because of financial issues. Whatever the case, whatever the reason, many marriages, I believe could have been much different, if the couples took the time to ask questions *before* getting married.

I remember a friend who married and desperately wanted to have children. After being married for a year, this friend was ready to have three children approximately one to two years apart. To my friend's dismay their spouse did not share the same vision. As a matter of fact, the spouse didn't want *any* children. That's right, *no* children! How did their messages get so crossed? How on earth could they not know that each other were so far apart in their views on having children? I'll tell you how. They didn't ask the question.

It is true that one could ask the question, receive an answer and later in the marriage the spouse changes their mind or reneges on their prior agreement. All in all, however, most people don't even take the time to ask in the first place. Many disagreements in marriage come about because the topic at hand was not brought up in conversation, fully discussed and decided upon. Don't let this happen to you.

What do I suggest? I suggest you interview your potential spouse. That's right, I said *interview*.

The concept of interviewing is not a new one. We interview people all the time. Usually when looking for a job, a potential employee will interview with a potential employer to see if a particular job will be a good match for the applying candidate. We interview people for admission into schools, solicited advice from experts on TV by interviewing them and even interview new cars and products to see if they will be best suited for our everyday needs. For some strange reason, when it comes to love, relationships and family we don't take as much time and care by interviewing our potential love interest. We spend less time deciding on a potential mate than we do in deciding to buy a car. This person is designed to spend *the rest of your life* with you. You are important enough to carve out more time to get to know this person (your potential mate) and get to know them well.

When I mention interview, I am referring to asking a series of questions over a period of time. I'm not talking about asking one or a few questions and then going about your life as usual. A good interviewer knows what to ask and when to ask it. The interviewer is careful to watch body language and is sensitive to how the person answers the questions. You must do the same. Ask many questions at different times and phrase them in a way that is not threatening but straightforward. I hope to write more on how to ask and what to ask, in another Wise Courtship book.

Earlier, I mentioned a friend whose marriage failed because they failed to ask the right questions before getting married. Just in case you are not convinced that asking questions beforehand could save a marriage, here are a couple more real life situations that destroyed or damaged certain marriages. The names have been changed to protect the identity of these people.

Case # 1 – Mr. & Mrs. Broke A. Lot

Clyde loved buying new things and showing them off. He would buy the latest and most expensive car, take exotic vacations and wear the latest fashions. Clyde loved doing these things because it afforded him the opportunity to show off to all his friends. He loved his women thin and beautiful because like all his possessions it would make him look good and he could brag to all of his acquaintances.

He really felt a sense of pride from what he had accumulated. When Clyde bought his house, his house cost at least $100,000 more than what his friends spent. It didn't matter whether it was worth that much or not, Clyde wanted to outdo everyone. Everything he had was top of the line even though he was sinking deeper and deeper in debt. When he met his wife, she was thin and beautiful, the essence of perfection. He showed pictures of her to all his friends and explained how perfect she was physically. There was never any talk about her mind or her character. She was beautiful on the outside and that was all that mattered.

Clyde's wife loved to spend money. She liked to look a certain way. She loved Clyde because he spared no expense. She blended in with his life well because she liked to take the exotic vacations and spend large. Clyde could brag; while she could get all the "goodies" she wanted. Everything was great until they married.

Well for the first few years, life was grand, until the bills mounted and the trips and gifts became few. When Clyde tried to get his wife to work, he found out she never really ever kept a job and never really intended to work. Ever! She had expected Clyde to support her whether they had children or not. Clyde was a laborer and was getting tired of lifting boxes and wanted relief from double overtime. His wife was tired of getting threatening phone calls from bill collectors and could not understand why Clyde didn't make enough. She had no idea what he did for a living. She knew he worked at a warehouse, but she didn't know that he was a laborer and she really had no clue what that meant totally in terms of pay, promotions or progression. Her dad was a doctor and he always took care of everything. She never really cooked before or cleaned and was used to being pampered.

With seemingly no help in sight, Clyde began to wonder about his marriage and his wife saw Clyde as a failure.

Case # 2 – Mr. & Mrs. A. Past

Tamara was the happiest woman in the world when Jaleel asked her to marry him. After all Jaleel was the most attractive man in their social circle. He was everything most women desire according to Tamara; tall, dark, handsome and had a job. He was the ladies' desire and he knew it. Jaleel loved the ladies and the ladies loved Jaleel. Who could resist his smile, charm, flashy dress and sense of adventure? The ladies naturally flocked to him. There wasn't a time Jaleel didn't have a lady on his arm. He never really had a long term relationship although he was now 50 years old. In fact, he really never spent too much time alone. He hated to be alone. He hadn't really discussed this with anyone except to a close buddy of his. Jaleel feels loved when surrounded by beautiful women. The women surrounding him tended to make wonderful comments about him that boosted his ego and made him feel great. He in turn had mastered the art of flattery but he was weak in commitment. Jaleel has an insatiable need for approval, to be desired and needed. He is temporarily satisfied through sexual pleasures and the initial phase of dating and falling in love. Once the relationship settles into a routine or a "working phase" of a relationship, better known as commitment, Jaleel loses interest. During this time, his partners were less flattering and flirtatious and desired a deeper long lasting love. Jaleel feels incompetent to share a true love. He is not sure what that is since he was abandoned by both his mother and father. It was too painful for Jaleel to even think about.

When Tamara came into Jaleel's life she was Jaleel's number one supporter and cheerleader. She loved saying and doing nice things for him because she secretly wanted him to return his affections in a similar way. She needed Jaleel and he loved that. Although Tamara grew up with both her parents they were neither affectionate nor supportive. Tamara's parents put her down and often ridiculed her. Tamara decided early on she would not be like her parents and adapted a very encouraging dialogue and lifestyle. Tamara was drawn to Jaleel's outward appearance and his flattering tongue since she felt inadequate in every way. Jaleel could be very attentive initially and Tamara longed for someone to take notice of her. Tamara was beautiful inside and out and surely she would supply Jaleel with the need of being wanted that he so desired. Jaleel was the epitome of success and surely Tamara's family would agree that she had done something right in her life.

After they were married life was wonderful for the first six months. Since both had an enormous need to be validated, neither one could ever really have their specific needs fulfilled. Jaleel became unfaithful and Tamara felt hurt, betrayed, unwanted and unloved. Consequently, their relationship ended in divorce.

I'm certain some of these case studies seem very unrealistic, but I assure you, they are not. You would be surprised at how many relationships flashed large, red flags along the way, only to be ignored. Notice these red flags, do the research and ask the right questions.

Interviewing your potential spouse brings about more marital satisfaction, less confusion and a closer bond.

Marital satisfaction

You are better off knowing what you are getting into rather than being surprised once you get into it. If you are expecting one thing out of your marriage and get another, the usual result is disappointment and dissatisfaction. Ask specific questions that pertain to issues that jeopardize your level of satisfaction in a marriage. Don't be shy in asking these types of questions. Your happiness is on the line.

If having a career is of utmost importance to you, you need to focus a lot of your questions around careers, what your opinion is on the subject and listen for their response to what you have said. What was your initial reaction to their response?

Decide together where the limits should be. Were you satisfied with what was decided? If not, you may want to rethink marriage, at least until common ground is found.

As one grows older, the amount of time to discover if a person is a great match for you should be less. The younger a person is, the longer it should take to discover if a potential spouse is a great match.

Less confusion

It goes without saying, that if you ask a question, discuss it and come to an agreement about an issue, that there will be less confusion in that area. There are times, however you can speak with someone and they do the exact opposite of what was agreed upon, but that occurrence is rare among rational people. Even when this is the case, repetitive discussions on the same issue can help to eliminate confusion and lessen the chance of a person saying one thing and doing another. The repeated conversations should happen *before* the marriage, however. (*If the person you are considering continues to say one thing and do another, this is a MAJOR RED FLAG! I suggest very strongly that you discontinue your relationship with this individual.*)

Start with the most important situations in your life and begin to ask questions related to that situation. Get as much clarity as possible from your potential spouse about how they feel and how you feel about the situation. Remember, there will be less confusion in your marriage if you do the initial work now.

In the case of my friend, a simple discussion beforehand could have saved their marriage unnecessary pain.

It's better to separate before marriage rather than separate after marriage.

Closer bond

Knowing your potential spouse's inner feelings, goals and desires can help to develop an unshakeable bond. No one should know your spouse better than you. You should be the first person they confide in, kick around ideas and discuss life challenges and issues with. Starting early, in particular before marriage to open the lines of communication can lay the foundation for a deep and lasting relationship. In the future, you may have to speak for your spouse when they are unable, support their causes or buffer them from unnecessary pain. These tasks become easier when you know them and know them well.

For many, beauty has become a more important quality when looking for a potential spouse. Of course we all want someone pleasing to the eye, but beauty in of itself will never bring the inner satisfaction that all humans seek. There are, I believe two voids in every human's life. One is the need for God and the other is a need to have a close, meaningful, long lasting relationship with another person. One void can only be filled through God alone. Many seek "flesh and blood" if you will, for constant companionship and there is certainly nothing wrong with that per se, but total satisfaction only comes from a relationship with Jesus Christ. As a matter of fact, if you or your potential spouse do not have a healthy relationship with Christ, nothing in this book, no counseling or "laying of hands" will be of much use.

Let's get back to the topic of beauty. Beauty alone will not fill those voids. You can have a beautiful spouse, but if that relationship is not meaningful and you do not feel needed, loved and wanted, you will not be fulfilled. If you get nothing else out of this book, I pray you got that. Beauty or anything else for that matter is a poor substitute for real honest to goodness love.

Get to know your potential spouse now and after you are married. Take an interest in what they are thinking and feeling. Discuss any and everything and commit to work all things out. It really makes the difference and it develops a closeness that words will never express.

Building this type of relationship is imperative because it reflects to the outside world Jesus the Christ's relationship to the church. *"Submit to one another out of reverence for Christ. Wives, submit yourselves to your own husbands as you do to the Lord. For the husband is the head of the wife as Christ is the head of the church, his body, of which he is the Savior. Now as the church submits to Christ, so also wives should submit to their husbands in everything. Husbands, love your wives, just as Christ loved the church and gave himself up for her to make her holy, cleansing her by the washing with water through the word, and to present her to himself as a radiant church, without stain or wrinkle or any other blemish, but holy and blameless. In this same way, husbands ought to love their wives as their own bodies. He who loves his wife loves himself. After all, no one ever hated their own body, but they feed and care for their body, just as Christ does the church— for we are members of his body. "For this reason a man will leave his father and mother and be united to his wife, and the two will become one flesh. "This is a profound mystery—but I am talking about Christ and the church."* (Ephesians 5:21-32, NIV)

We are walking examples of how Christ interacts with His people. What types of example will we or are we showing?

When you are sure you have asked all the questions you could possibly ask; the next step will be to observe your potential spouse.

For possible questions to ask a potential spouse, check out my upcoming book "Wise Courtship: Q & A." For more information, visit, www.WiseCourtship.com .

People who are successful in an area think differently than the norm. Get inside of their thinking and replicate.

'For this reason a man will leave his father and mother and be united to his wife,

Mark 10:7

What you see is what you get

Okay, you have carefully selected the exact questions you must have answers to before committing yourself to anyone. You have even gone so far as to make notes once you got home as to what your potential spouse said to you. This person answered each question exactly the way you wanted them to. They definitely seem to be Mr. or Mrs. Right. Right? Wrong. You have only gotten to first base. The second step is to observe them *and* observe them, without them knowing it.

Please don't misunderstand me. I am not suggesting that you "stalk" the person you are interested in. There is a distinct difference between stalking and observing. When you stalk someone, you are peeping into another's life uninvited, intrusively and uncomfortably. Wikipedia defines stalking as a term commonly used to refer to unwanted and obsessive attention by an individual or group to another person. Stalking behaviors are related to harassment and intimidation and may include following the victim in person and/or monitoring them. If you find yourself sitting in a car, without your potential mate knowing and glaring at their every move or waiting for them to arrive or leave, you may be stalking. Seek help.

Seeing is believing

Observing however requires that you watch your partner in their natural settings. You are invited and not a stalker, because you will observe while on dates and outings. If you spend most of your time together, kissing, touching and having sex you may have a tough time with this exercise. Although those activities may be fun, they also consume time and they don't leave much opportunity to actually get to *know* the person. You really do want to know if this person is a hatchet murder or not! Remember having sex before marriage is an activity we should avoid. *"But among you there must not be even a hint of sexual immorality, or of any kind of impurity, or of greed, because these are improper for God's holy people. Nor should there be obscenity, foolish talk or coarse joking, which are out of place, but rather thanksgiving. For of this you can be sure: No immoral, impure or greedy person—such a person is an idolater—has any inheritance in the kingdom of Christ and of God."* (Ephesians 3:3-5, NIV)

Also note: *"It is God's will that you should be sanctified: that you should avoid sexual immorality; that each of you should learn to control your own body in a way that is holy and honorable, not in passionate lust like the pagans, who do not know God; and that in this matter no one should wrong or take advantage of a brother or sister. The Lord will punish all those who commit such sins, as we told you and warned you before. For God did not call us to be impure, but to live a holy life."* (1 Thessalonians 4:3-7, NIV)

Having sex or routine petting and kissing before knowing someone well, can distort your view of this person. I can't tell you how many times I or others have tried to alert our friends of their boy or girlfriend's character only to be sent away and told to shut up. Why? We were sent away because our friends were emotionally or should I say sexually or lustfully involved to see their choice for what they truly were. Do yourself a favor and look before you leap or lust!

Case # 3 – Jerome's Judgment

Jerome was a great guy. He was a hard worker, attended church regularly and tried to do right by everyone. He had a wonderful girlfriend who was set to soon be his wife until he met Lola. There was nothing particularly outstanding about Lola. Jerome wasn't attracted to her and quite frankly opposed her views and was disgusted by her behavior. Lola however was able to win Jerome over by her flattering words which ultimately led to a sexual relationship. He hadn't had a sexual relationship with his fiancé. He knew it was wrong to continue to see Lola, but always believed he would come back to his fiancé. Having sex with Lola clouded Jerome's judgment. He was in so deep, that Lola was able to talk Jerome into marrying her. After all he was a Christian and had stepped over the line and should rectify his mistakes by marrying her, so he thought. There were so many opportunities for Jerome to back out of his decision before marrying Lola, but he rationalized within himself why his decision to marry someone he didn't love and to abandon his fiancé was correct. Besides he had become a leader in the church and most of the congregants have seen him with Lola. If he left her now there may be some embarrassment, possibly ramifications. What would the church say? It was much easier to pretend than to admit he was wrong and try to correct his mistakes. He ignored all of God's warnings to end this relationship and go back to his fiancé.

The end result was a tumultuous marriage from the very beginning, the raising of very unhappy children and a daily decision whether or not to stay married to his wife. He now suffers physical ailments from all the stress this marriage has caused.

Having sex too soon disturbed Jerome's ability to *see* Lola for what she was. It is hard to imagine that most of Jerome's troubles started from a decision to have premarital sex.

In addition, having sex outside of marriage as indicated in the scriptures mentioned earlier, sends a terrible example of how one should live in the world. Is the example you are setting encouraging others to live for Christ? Is God's way better? I believe so. Do you? If so, show it.

In this next case study, Patzy's mistake of participating in premarital sex causes a destructive pattern or cycle in her life.

Case # 4 – Patzy's Patch Ups

Patzy like most teenagers felt she knew more than her parents. Although she had been raised in church and knew the teachings of the Bible, Patzy decided to live life her own way. Patzy was intrigued by a fast talking older man who flashed cash wherever he went. It never dawned on her to ask why he was always home and never seemed to work. It's an old story. Patzy became pregnant and the family forced the man to marry her. Since he never kept a job, she had to work while pregnant day and night, while unknowingly to her he was involved in criminal activity. She finally left him, but began dating another man soon after her marriage fell apart. Once she became pregnant by this new man she married him. After all, her philosophy was to be married to the man she became pregnant by. There was no thought to prescreening a potential spouse, withhold sex until after marriage and then have children.

This marriage was even worse than the first with many children being conceived in those years. Of course, this marriage ended. Before this marriage was completely over, Patzy met another man. The courtship was extremely short leaving no time to get to know him. After getting pregnant by the third man she married him quickly. This man turned out to be a loser as well and an abuser of her children. Patzy met another man and became pregnant by him. As tradition would have it, she married. The marriage was a flop, but Patzy is older now and feels she should live with her decision and just go on with life. She is miserable, but medicates the pain by attending church three to four times daily.

Patzy never gave herself a chance to see any of these men for what they were due to premature sexual relationships.

Case # 5 – Wanda's Wildlife

Wanda was overweight. Although she was funny, intelligent, hardworking, a great friend and so much more, her self-esteem was low. She just didn't feel good about herself because of her weight.

Wanda tried everything to lose the weight but couldn't. She wasn't trying to lose weight for health reasons; she wanted to lose the weight to reflect the images she had seen in magazines. She thought if she could just look like the models she saw in magazines she would attract someone who she could have a relationship with.

When her efforts failed, she began to develop loud speech, loud laughter and an all-around loud and wild lifestyle. Wanda yearned for attention and did whatever to get it. She drank, used drugs, had sex with anyone and hung out all hours of the night. The more she lived this wild lifestyle, the lonelier she became. She never reached her goal of marriage and family because the decisions she made took her further and further from the people, places and circumstances that could have helped her reach her goal. Instead Wanda lives alone, has one grown child, is bitter and continues to live a promiscuous life believing marriage and family is a dream for the foolish.

Case # 6 – Matthew's Matchmaker Mess

Matthew was determined to be a success. He experienced tough times growing up and was anxious to make his life better than it had been. As a politician he could help others and himself as well. Matthew studied successful politicians and tried to replicate what many had done before him. He noticed that many were married and he was determined to get a wife to "jump start" his career.

For the most part, Matthew married the first girl he connected with from his small hometown. She was young and right out of high school. Jean, his wife had very low self-esteem. She was jealous of everything including Matthew's friends, his career and just about everyone she came in contact with. Jean's perception about people and life was much distorted. She believed people were always talking about her or that people thought they were better than her. This stopped Jean from accompanying her husband to functions and when she did, she would cause a scene.

Jean had her high school diploma but felt no match for those with Bachelors, Masters and Doctorate degrees. Instead of bettering herself she complained. She failed to cook, keep the house clean and/or seek employment.

Matthew and Jean managed to have children, but they were unkept, unloved and unwanted. Jean had no drive in life whatsoever and spent her days, emptying out the bank account, smoking, drinking and having affairs. Her behavior began to cause trouble in Matthew's career. After a scandalous affair involving Jean became public, Matthew divorced Jean but suffered many years of Jean's antics and the dysfunction that played out in their children's lives.

The examples mentioned previously, help to serve as examples of how involving one's self in sex, money, having a good time or someone's looks can skew your ability to observe. In order to observe with optimum results, you need to observe your potential mate in a variety of settings. This means you will be DATING. Go skating, bowling, to dinner or horseback riding. Meet their parents. Accompany them to their family reunion and to church, formal affairs and business activities. (If invited, this is to assume you are invited to these events. If not invited, why? Ask YOURSELF this question, not your potential spouse. Again we are not trying to establish a strained, controlling relationship. You are only asking yourself this question to develop a clear picture of where your relationship, if any stands.) The more you observe the better. This is why interviewing them first is so important. You don't want to spend a lot of time with someone who doesn't seem to share the same interests and life goals you do.

Seek and ye shall find

What am I looking for? Everything. Don't be cynical and don't turn into "Inspector Gadget". Enjoy yourself and just pay attention to see if what your potential mate told you in the interview phase is what they are *actually* living in their life. Did they say they were shy, but actually they are the life of the party? This may not mean much, but it may, to you.

Many issues can be discussed, but some situations can only be observed in everyday life situations. How does this person really handle money? Do they use a credit card for everything? How often do they purchase items in a single day? What type of items? Again, I'm not asking you to be nosey, just pay attention. Be aware so that you are not totally shocked by your potential spouse actions later on.

Make sure to observe areas in their life that are of importance to you. For instance, if you feel the person needs to have a job, make sure they are working. Have you actually seen their place of employment? Have you met co-workers? What type of worker are they? How long have they been with the company? While the answers to these questions may not insure the validity of your findings, observing the answers to these questions help to insure a more solid foundation in your growing relationship.

Case # 7 – Unsteady Freddie is a Flop

When Mary met Freddie she thought she met the man of her dreams. He was perfect in every way except she did notice he was often late, irresponsible and had a lackadaisical approach to everything. When Mary asked Freddie about his employment, Freddie shared that he worked at a department store for three years. In addition, Freddie was living with a relative and it never crossed Mary's mind to inquire why, at Freddie's age, he had been living with this relative for over ten years. In fact, he had lived with friends or family members all his life and never had a place of his own. Freddie never paid rent or mortgage payments, electric, water or any bill for that matter. Of course much later, Mary learned that Freddie was an unsteady house guest who often ran up expenses and failed to contribute in any way.

Mary never took her friend's advice about checking into Freddie's employment. It wasn't until after they were married she found out that Freddie did not work for the department store for three consecutive years. He indeed was working for the store, but it had been on a temporary base for a couple months at a time, sporadically. Not only that, he often lost jobs due to laziness, being late and petty crimes.

Freddie, once married to Mary continued his tradition of laziness, lack of work; lack of responsibility and unfortunately, petty crimes.

It goes without saying that asking the right questions can help you get to know a person. Observing them in many different situations can solidify what you *think* you know, but researching or investigating what you *heard* and *saw* can sift out the real from the fake.

For more information on this topic, check out my upcoming book "Wise Courtship: See it, Believe it." For more information, visit, www.WiseCourtship.com .

Take the time to know what you are getting.

'and the two will become one flesh.' So they are no longer two, but one flesh.

Mark 10:8

Let the buyer beware

There is an old Latin phrase that says "Caveat Emptor" which simply means: *Let the buyer beware*! Although we are not purchasing a spouse, there are many expectations we place on one another that are similar to those we place on purchased items. We want to know that when we purchase an item, it will perform the task as advertised. We are NOT purchasing anyone, but we DO want to know if this potential spouse measures up to what is being advertised. Investigate through outside sources to check your facts about this person. This step is vital; because it brings together information that you have asked directly and saw with your own eyes. The final step in the Wise Courtship system is investigation.

Check it or forget it

What do you mean, matching up to what is being advertised? When we court, date, or go out with a potential spouse we are advertising ourselves all the time. The way we wear our hair, the manner of dress, what we say and what we do are all examples of advertising. Your mission, if you choose to accept it, is to see if what is being advertised, matches up with what has been said and what has been seen. If every time you see your potential spouse they have a new hairdo that has been professionally done, you may want to reflect on prior conversations and observations. Does this behavior line up with what has been said about their finances? Does it line up with your expectations? There is nothing wrong with a professional hairdo. There is a problem if it bothers you and doesn't line up with what you two have been discussing. It may also be a problem if a person gets their hair done professionally frequently. Hairdos were really a crazy example, but I hope you got the point. Also note that their hair may be professionally done or just *appears* to be. It may have been done by them. Getting their hair done *may* appear that they are overspending when they told you they do not overspend. However, if the is fact they did their hair themselves and it *looks* professionally done, you may have gathered misinformation. Investigation helps to alleviate misinformation. This is why each step of the Wise Courtship system is so important; interview, observe and investigate/research. The combination of these steps help to get a clearer picture of what you are dealing with.

Remember we are seeking outside sources in our research/investigate phase. So the hairdo example would be a little different. For instance, you find out through relatives, colleagues and passersby (kidding) that your potential spouse gets professional hairdos every day spending $200 for each hairdo. This does not line up with what they told you about spending frugally. This is a red flag. Red flags in a relationship tell us to stop. Stop and get clarification. Stop and get help. Stop and get out. We should stop and do one or all of the previously mentioned.

I'm sure I have made myself as clear as mud, but let's proceed, shall we?

Case # 8 – Bad Bertina

Dustin was excited about marrying Bertina. During their very short time together she seemed to have a bubbly personality and was a lot of fun to be around. She always laughed and smiled and pushed aside chores to be with him. Dustin instantly trusted her since they were from the same hometown and figured Bertina shared the same values as he did. Bertina was very flirtatious and it made Dustin feel loved and wanted. He was attracted to Bertina and they shared an undeniable chemistry. They spent most of their time hugging, kissing and petting and virtually no time discussing topics and issues that were of importance or should have been in their budding relationship. Instead of taking more time to get to know Bertina, Dustin rushed to marry her. They both were very young.

After they were married, Dustin was surprised to learn that Bertina did not cook or clean as *HE* expected. As a matter of fact, she demanded "take out", often "fast food" restaurants every day for all three meals. She was a horrible housekeeper, keeping clothes, food and dirt all over the place. Often they or their guests would have to force and push the front door open because of all the junk that blocked their pathway. Dustin was moving up in the business and couldn't invite anyone to his home because of the condition of his house. Bertina was home all day but never took time or pride in keeping the house clean, working with the children, cooking or building a career. If Bertina had done any or all of the above, Dustin would have been satisfied.

Bertina continued her flirtatious ways after being married, however her attentions were directed at other men. Bertina had endless affairs with these men in front of her children, family and friends.

Dustin was disgusted and often wondered how his relationship turned out so bad. What had he missed? He quickly realized there were many hints and signs to how Bertina *would* or *may* act in the future, but he ignored them all. He wouldn't allow himself to see what he saw or investigate the validity of his findings.

Better to be safe than sorry

Here are some outside sources that should be tapped into when taking further investigation of a potential spouse:

- Friends/Family
- Co-workers/Colleagues
- Law enforcement
- Medical professionals
- Financial informers or information

This list can vary. There may be more or less outside sources utilized depending on the circumstances.

When one looks at the above list, it may seem a little much to want to speak with your potential spouse about finances or research that area. However, over 80% of divorces ended because of finances. You may not be able to find out many particulars, but you will hear about their character if you take the time to pay attention without any unnecessary probing. I am not suggesting that you make an appointment with their financial advisor, nor visit the advisor without your potential spouse's knowledge. It is just a source that *can* be tapped into when deemed necessary by both you *and* your potential spouse. Financial informers can range from advisors, creditors to average people who your potential spouse owes money or may have lent money to. The point is to be knowledgeable in that area and to do your research. Most of the information gathered should come through a casual meeting with your potential spouse. Again, I am not advocating intrusive or offensive prying.

There will be a window of time when you are about to go into marriage (engagement) when a formal meeting with your potential spouse *and* the financial advisor will be necessary. At this stage of the relationship, the research phase, you will be allowed a deeper look into your potential spouse's life and you must get as much information at this stage as possible. If your relationship has gotten as far as engagement, you need to be a little more courageous in your fact finding.

Importance of premarital counseling

If you have not done so already, please take a moment and read the Forward of this book. The Forward was written by Cora Jakes-Coleman the daughter of Bishop T.D. Jakes, Pastor of The Potters House in Dallas, Texas. Mrs. Coleman writes about how premarital counseling helped her in preparing for her marriage.

In essence, this book helps to serve as a tool in premarital counseling. However, there are many benefits to sitting down with your Pastor or counselor to share, learn and discuss. A Pastor, counselor or third party will be able to pick up cues from the both of you from your body language, verbiage, moods and so on. Whereas your potential spouse can avoid answering questions or sharing with you, it becomes difficult to do so with someone else is in the room. A Pastor or counselor can be objective and see what happens or hear what is actually being said. When we are close to someone we tend to make allowances for their behavior whether right or wrong. A great premarital counselor will address what needs to be addressed and not "sugar coat" anything.

Premarital counseling is invaluable. Take advantage of it. Proverbs 15: 22 teaches, *"Plans fail for lack of counsel, but with many advisers they succeed."* (NIV) Choose your counselors and advisors wisely.

When looking for someone to counsel you and your potential spouse look for qualified people. Have they counseled before? What is their educational background or credentials? Consider their spiritual maturity. Is it evident in their life that they are exercising biblical principles? Is their marriage successful? Their marriage does not have to be problem free, but have they shown a history of "stick to it ness"?

There is much debate on whether someone who has been divorced can offer premarital counseling. Keep this in mind. Those who are successful at something can tell us *how* to do it. Those who are not successful in an area can tell us *what went wrong* or what *not* to do. Although I do not suggest a divorced person give premarital counseling as a rule, if the individual comes from one of the perspectives mentioned earlier, they can be very helpful to you. Make sure the individual does not have a "tainted" or cynical view of relationships and marriage. Their views can affect your view. Proceed in caution.

For your consideration

As an aside, if you are reading this book after the fact, meaning you already are engaged or living with someone, don't skip the interview or observation phase. The first two phases are vital. They will tell you without a doubt, if you really know this person you have married. You'll be glad you took the time. Trust me. It's never too late, to get it straight!

There is much debate on whether one should "live" with their potential spouse before marriage or not. I do not believe this is a good idea nor is it necessary. "Living" with someone is much like a "look and see" or "rent to own" situation. While you are living a mock marriage life, you discover idiosyncrasies about each other that cause you not to want to marry this person. Much like living in a home before you buy it, you hear all the creeks and see all the cracks within. You are convinced you can buy better elsewhere. The process of "living" with someone gives a "way out" to leave whenever one feels they are unsatisfied with their partner. It does not encourage commitment. Let's face it, no one is perfect, not even you.

You find out many things about a person once living with them that you would not know otherwise. However, you can find out just as much as I have stated throughout this book by interviewing, observing and investigating. One may argue, can we find out if someone is a murder, abuser, embezzler or drunk? I believe you can. In addition, I believe we see signs about a person and often ignore them. We usually don't ask the questions necessary, or talk to the right people about our suspicions.

There are some details we will never know about a person until married. In fact, it may be a total surprise to your partner as well that they do some of the things they do. These details if you really love the person and are not illegal, ill moral or harmful can be overlooked or rectified. Once knowing the inner person, small flaws can be overlooked and covered in love. We all need to be loved just for who we are and once you have done your work up front, enjoy them and celebrate their uniqueness.

If you just "live" with someone and skip the steps in this book, you will join many others in a "merry-go-round" of love affairs one after the other, never experiencing deep, committed and lasting love.

Let's go back and look at the list mentioned before again. The first two outside sources are a must. These sources are easy to tap into and are usually readily available.

Talk with family and friends

I can't tell you how many people I know who have committed themselves to long term relationships and never met the other person's family. You may be surprised at the information that can be derived during a visit with your mate's loved ones. Some information can be obtained simply by observing. Of course some information can be answered by asking a direct question.

While visiting a girlfriend of mine, a young lady who was dating my girlfriend's brother asked my girlfriend to give an honest evaluation of her brother. My girlfriend turned to her and said, "My brother is a dog!" I was shocked my girlfriend told this lady the truth with no reservations whatsoever. The young lady just laughed it off and said, "Really! Stop joking!" My girlfriend assured her that she was not joking and added that her brother could not be trusted and was a womanizer. (Basically what she was saying was that he is a dog.)

What in us makes us want to ignore what is right in front of us? Not everything you see is what it appears to be, but it can reveal a great portion of what may be going on. Take it seriously and consider.

There is a chance that what you view at a family gathering may be terribly skewed. During bereavement for instance, the family visited may be extremely sad, irritable or off kilter in some way. This is natural of course. However, unless there are some extenuating circumstances, what you witness with your eyes among family and friends of your potential mate is vital and must be taken seriously.

Time and time again many have stated that they are marrying their spouse and not the family. This is simply not true. There are very few people who live totally separate from family and close friends. In general, most people are deeply intertwined with their family whether the relationship is good or bad.

In an ideal situation, marrying into a family with a loving and supportive bond is optimal. What happens if the family members hate each other or there are toxic relationships throughout? No one chooses the family they are born into. We cannot control the actions of each family member or close friend. Look for how your mate *handles* their relationship with the family member. If the relationship is toxic or abusive has it ended? Is your mate in an unhealthy relationship and unwilling or unequipped to get out? These are questions to consider and many other questions should be considered before moving ahead in your courtship. How these issues are resolved or not resolved for that matter **WILL** affect you. Investigate.

Mingle with co-workers and business associates

Those who work with us see us from a prospective that many may not have the opportunity to. Their view of us in most cases is objective. In addition, getting your potential spouse out in the open can give you a chance to determine their public image, give others a chance to see and evaluate and comment on your choice. I am not suggesting that your partner is on display but you shouldn't hide them. Bring them into the light for a closer view by all. Secrets linger in the dark. Read on and you'll understand why I made the "secrets lingering in the dark" comment.

Welcome your co-workers' feedback and keep an open mind. You may be surprised by their response and it may even save your life.

Take Amber Frey for instance. She met Scott Peterson who by the way was using an alias without Amber Frey's knowledge. She had sexual relations with him after hours of knowing him and introduced him to her 20-month old daughter all in less than a week. It was once said that it wasn't until she took Scott Peterson to a dinner party and introduced him to friends and associates that one of them grew suspicious and "Googled" some form of information on him. Because of that simple search, it was revealed that Scott Peterson was a main suspect in his wife Laci Peterson and unborn child's murder. The name he had given to Amber Frey was not actually his name. The relationship between Scott Peterson and Amber Frey was a lie. Scott Peterson was a liar and worse of all, he was a murder suspect. Later, Scott Peterson was arrested for murder as he tried to escape to another country.

What is known is that the friend of Amber Frey who introduced her to Scott Peterson later found out Scott was married through this friend's coworker. Scott Peterson's alibi was that he was a widow and the memories were too painful to share with Amber. The friend convinced him that he should confess to Amber about his marriage. As we now know Scott had much more to confess to Amber. Whichever scenario actually happened or happened first, it is frightening what can occur when attempting to build a relationship with someone. Ms. Frey was very fortunate indeed to have friends to intervene in either case.

What a scary but true example of how important it is and how valuable it can be to bring your partner around co-workers and business associates. One of these associates did the investigation Amber Frey failed to do and it ultimately saved her life.

Law enforcement / medical professionals

I'm sure after seeing this section of the book you may believe I have gone mad, bonkers or crazy, but I assure you I have not. Most information can be gathered about an individual through a series of conversations. It is through the conversations that one may either hear or see something that will require further research. This does not mean snooping but you do need to know if you've got your facts straight. When in causal relationship a conversation might do, but as the relationship gets more serious, you need to observe and seek further information as well.

It is my belief that if you feel you must snoop or do an in-depth investigation on anyone; you may want to rethink this relationship. Your instincts are usually correct. If you have suspicions about an individual and you have bought into those suspicions, your relationship may not be on solid ground. The evidence or what seems to be evidence can be in of itself enough to call it quits.

In our present society one has to be so careful. In the Amber Frey example above, one may feel that this could never happen to them. Amber Frey may have thought this as well, but was very wrong. What if Scott Peterson was a sexual predator and harmed her little girl? It is not being too cautious in wanting to know someone's criminal history if any. It can save you a lot of irreversible heartache and damage.

Let's face it, times have changed. You can no longer take anything for granted. For instance, are you really sure your partner is the gender they claim or seem to be? Just asking. Do they have a criminal record? Are they a sexual predator? Do they have addictions? Are they a bigot? Do they make bombs in their bedroom in their spare time?

In regards to your potential spouse's health, you have the right to know before marrying, if this person has health issues especially chronic ones. Do they have diabetes, a terminal illness or AIDS? Can they have children? Are they impotent? Have they been under psychiatric care? It's okay if a person has a medical past or present but you need to know.

Determine person's public image

What is your partner like in public? This question will be the base of your investigation. Remember, this entire book was designed to help you determine if this person, your potential spouse is the right fit for *you*. So if you are comfortable with the fact he or she eats with their toes; that is fine with me. The point is not to move so quickly through the relationship and later after marriage discover they eat with their toes and want a divorce.

What type of behavior are you comfortable with from your partner in a public setting? Listen, the person is who they are. You cannot change them so what you see is truly what you will get.

You may desire a "life of the party" type or one that is more refined. What are others' opinions of your potential spouse's public image?

Determine person's private image

Unfortunately, some people are one way in public and the other way in private. It's possible they can be loving to you in front of other people and abusive to you in private. This is never a good situation. Their treatment of you should remain constant. If you are being abused in any way in your relationship get out and seek help.

Sometimes people may be the opposite at home due to the work or position they may hold in the public world. If your partner holds a very public position, such as politicians, speakers, pastors, entertainers and the like, they may be very quiet at home although they are very verbal in public. A change in behavior such as this may not cause alarm. Working all day speaking and greeting people can be tiring and your partner may just want to retreat and relax during their private moments with you, family and close friends.

Tally your results

Once you have asked as many questions as possible, observed with your own eyes your partner's actions and researched further some of your findings, it's now time to add up your results. I know this sound as if I am asking you to be extremely scientific about love which can be totally emotional, but tallying your results does not have to be as "cold" as it seems. I'm sure there are some who benefit from sitting down and making a list of the pros and cons of what they have discovered about their potential spouse, but it does not have to be that structured. You could resolve in your mind what to do with what you know by relaxing alone and taking time to think it over. Friends and family members can help to give an objective opinion. Talking with a Pastor or counselor can also be beneficial. Pray alone. The point is to take serious time to reflect and make sure this person is right for you. Biblically speaking, once the decision is made to marry this person, there is no turning back.

For more information on this topic, check out my upcoming book "Wise Courtship: Dig Deeper." For more information, visit, www.WiseCourtship.com .

All that glitters is not gold. Be careful falling in love with the outside package; what a person looks like or what they appear to be, it may be false advertisement

"Therefore what God has joined together, let not one separate."

Mark 10:9

No refunds, no returns

This book, in its entirety has been about what to look for while in courtship with another. Paying close attention to signs, investigating them and asking the right questions are strongly advised BEFORE marriage. Do the work up front, now before getting married for your best chance of happiness.

What if they won't talk?

If you try to get to know your potential spouse and they won't open up and talk with you, take this as a serious sign. Either they have something to hide or they have trust issues. Whatever the case, it will take quite a bit of heartache to get to know them. It is best to leave these types of people alone. Their needs are beyond your expertise and besides you are not running a rehabilitation, recovery or restoration center. If this person has issues, leave them alone to work it out on their own. You cannot change anyone or force them to seek help.

There are many other people who are willing to connect with you and love you. Get out. Do things. Meet people and you will encounter them.

The challenged life

There will be many challenges and obstacles you will face once married. If you try hard in the beginning to know your potential spouse and to make sure you are happy with your choice, facing challenges together in marriage will become easier.

My husband and I faced a very tragic situation in our life. Initially it required great faith from me and a strong belief in his character. This became easy because of former conversations, observations and you guessed it, looking into what I learned prior to marriage. Because of his candid conversations *before* marriage, we were able to get through a very tough and tumultuous time *during* marriage. Utilizing the techniques outlined in this book will help to develop a bond that will be difficult if not impossible to break.

Marriage is supposed to last forever. With this in mind, who will you spend your forever with?

For more information on this topic, check out my upcoming book "Wise Courtship: Revelation." For more information, visit, www.WiseCourtship.com .

This book has attempted to assist you in discovering if your potential spouse is really right for you. Please know that GOD should be the only one who puts couples together. Often we pick who we want without consulting GOD. We don't ask GOD "is this person who you want for me?" This book is intended to step you through this process to discover or confirm GOD'S choice in your life. If you listen to GOD, you will NEVER go wrong.

Toni realizing the awesome calling of matrimony.

Toni shares first dance with husband Brian.

Cora with husband Richard Brandon Coleman.

Cora with sister Sarah and mom, First Lady Serita Jakes

Cora with her father Bishop T.D. Jakes Pastor of the Potters House in Dallas, TX.

Bishop Jakes prays over the couple.

Cora enjoying the day with new husband family and friends.

A wedding gift

The following is a list of individuals who specialize in pre-marital counseling. The list was taken from the Focus on the Family database. I am not endorsing any of these counselors. It is up to you to check credentials and gather testimonials on their services. This list is being supplied for reference purposes only.

For more information, visit on the source of this list, visit www.focusonthefamily.com .

Alabama

E. Haygood
Birmingham Alabama 35209
205-879-7500

Sallie Lowman
Birmingham Alabama 35242
205-408-2787

Bonnie Roberts
Birmingham Alabama 35243
205-977-3003

Tommy Smith
Brewton Alabama 36426
251-809-3191

Jack Camilleri
Daphne Alabama 36526
251-625-1480

Pamela Garner
Huntsville Alabama 35803
256-426-9009

Bonnie Hill
Mobile Alabama 36695
251-604-1733

Martha Sullins
Mobile Alabama 36695
251-633-2122

Robert Hunt
Montgomery Alabama 36109
334-303-5594

L. Donald Hill
Montgomery Alabama 36117
334-272-8622

Robert Parsons
Ozark Alabama 36360
334-790-5649

Craig Boden
Rainbow City Alabama 35906
256-442-5757

Alaska

Richard Clampitt
Wasilla Alaska 99654
907-376-0776

Arizona

Dallas Demmitt
Gilbert Arizona 85233
480-497-0077

Nancy Demmitt
Gilbert Arizona 85233
480-497-0077

Chris Andersen
Glendale Arizona 85308

623-680-8172

Marian Eberly
Phoenix Arizona 85029
623-252-7433

Joan Cook
Phoenix Arizona 85029
602-548-8508

Deborah Tyrrell
Phoenix Arizona 85050
602-402-5034

Laurie Tetreault
Prescott Arizona 86303
928-771-9422 ext 3

Larry Messer
Scottdale Arizona 85258
480-332-4281

Zona Gregory
Scottdale Arizona 85260
480-451-0488

Gregory Crow
Scottsdale Arizona 85251
480-947-1989

William Johnson
Sedona Arizona 86351
928-774-7302

Tad Skinner
Tempe Arizona 85281
480-363-8858

William Seery
Tucson Arizona 85705
520-461-0028

Maureen Brand
Tucson Arizona 85742
520-579-6682

Vern McNally
Wickenburg Arizona 85390
602-944-4120

California

Donelyn Miller
Aptos California 95003
831-460-2550 ext. #3

Brent Patterson
Bishop California 93514
760-872-4099

Vicki Harvey
Brea California 92821
714-529-5712

Judith Van Bebber
Brea California 92821
714-615-1400

Sue Burkeen
Brentwood California 94513
925-513-3128

Elaine With
Brentwood California 94513
925-937-1245

Sylvia Ching
Brentwood California 94513
925-301-5369

Mary Scholten
Buena Park California 90620
714-883-3593

Jackie Rittenhouse
Camarillo California 93010
805-216-6445

Diane Boll
Corona California 92879
951-377-2138

Patricia Canepa
Corona California 92879
949-262-7828

Walt Becker
Coronado California 92118

619-435-7791

Burdetta Honescko
Costa Mesa California 92626
714-998-1914

Scott Logan
Costa Mesa California 92626
949-275-6735

Kimberly Clark
Costa Mesa California 92626
714-614-7382

Max Kayes
Covina California 91724
951-247-6542 ext. 250

Jeenie Gordon
Covina California 91724
626-967-6421 ext. 203

Chris Love
Crestline California 92325
909-810-6426

Laura Taggart
Danville California 94526
925-820-1467

Timothy Geare
Del Mar California 92014
858-436-4275

Gina Taffi
Del Mar California 92014
858-699-8011

Gary Hittle
El Centro California 92243
760-355-8404

Cynthia Winn
Encino California 91436
818-789-3346

David Ferreira
Escondido California 92025
760-489-0598

Susan Garland
Fountain Valley California 92708
714-965-2040

Marilyn Kirkwood
Fresno California 93711
559-221-8874

Ruth Graybill
Fullerton California 92835
562-903-4799 ext. 5403#

Cindy Greenslade
Garden Grove California 92845
714-403-7356

Laura Venable
Gold River California 95670
916-492-7900

Cynthia Munz
Gold River California 95670
916-658-9990

Bob Parkins
Gold River California 95670
916-337-5406

G. Brian Jones
Grass Valley California 95949
530-268-1146

Max Kayes
Hemet California 92544
951-247-6542 ext. 250

Trang Leete
Huntington Beach California 92647
714-369-0932

Christine Brown
Huntington Beach California 92648
714-717-2521

William Gaultiere
Irvine California 92604
949-413-8610

Kristi Gaultiere

Irvine California 92604
949-293-8273

Susan Harris
La Habra California 90631
562-690-4060

Pamela Luschei
La Mesa California 91941
619-460-8500

Nora Klemenz
La Mesa California 91941
619-994-5989

William Graff
La Mesa California 91941
619-589-8971

Charles Long
La Mesa California 91942
619-462-0199

Yovana Munro
La Mesa California 91942
619-368-8617

Gary Hittle
La Mesa California 91942
619-464-7771

Ruth Graybill
La Mirada California 90638
562-903-4799 ext. 5403#

Piper Glasier
Laguna Hills California 92653
949-443-2222

Larry Hamilton
Laguna Hills California 92653
949-707-1613

Leah Hamilton
Laguna Hills California 92653
949-707-5788

Patricia Canepa
Laguna Niguel California 92677
949-262-7828

Nacera Matallah
Lake Forest California 92630
714-601-1270

Mary Simms
Long Beach California 90807
562-984-2012

Cheryl Jones-Dix
Long Beach California 90807
562-493-9089

Sheila Bost
Los Angeles California 90025
310-317-1615

Nan Dhuet
Los Angeles California 90041
323-908-6119

Sari Sheppard
Los Angeles California 90064
310-826-4300

Edward Brackenbury
Menlo Park California 94025
650-324-0619

Eugene Whitney
Mission Viejo California 92691
949-582-2492

Max Kayes
Moreno Valley California 92553
951-247-6542 ext. 250

Peter Petsas
Moreno Valley California 92553
909-289-4217

Jean Galica
Morgan Hill California 95037
408-644-3294

Robert Wright
Murrieta California 92562
951-304-0882 ext 3

Max Kayes

Murrieta California 92562
951-247-6542 ext. 250

Ronald Rowe
National City California 91950
619-327-0315

Patricia Canepa
Newport Beach California 92660
949-262-7828

Mark MacMillin
Newport Beach California 92660
714-420-3704

Scott Williams
Northridge California 91324
818-701-0107

Wendy Williams
Northridge California 91324
818-701-0107

Jolinda Thomas
Oakhurst California 93644
559-641-6321

Kristofer Anderson
Ontario California 91761
909-262-1768

David Smith
Orange California 92866
714-324-2209

Robyn Bettenhausen
Orange California 92868
714-558-9266

Edward Brackenbury
Palo Alto California 94303
650-302-0546

Sam Alibrando
Pasadena California 91101
626-577-8303

Margaret Guy
Pasadena California 91101
626-449-5639

Jeffery Bjorck
Pasadena California 91101
626-584-5530

Richard Rupp
Pasadena California 91101
626-449-1419

Bonnie Summers
Pleasant Hill California 94523
925-890-7651

Sue Burkeen
Pleasanton California 94588
925-513-3128

Doris Dea
Pleasanton California 94588
925-472-2556

Roger Seymour
Rancho Cucamonga California 91701
909-980-4137

Catherine Seymour
Rancho Cucamonga California 91701
909-980-4137

Lori Lira
Rancho Mirage California 92270
760-989-1898

Rodney Dean
Rancho Mirage California 92270
760-568-6789

Barry Byrne
Redding California 96001
530-242-5848

Don Ostendorf
Redding California 96001
530-241-5999

Jason Carr
Redlands California 92373
909-206-2141

Royce Garvin

Redwood California 94061
650-368-0210

Beth Baus
Riverside California 92504
951-682-1153

Lisa Willmon
Riverside California 92506
951-320-1390

Gregory Wohl
Riverside California 92506
951-544-1157

Lu Ann Ahrens
Riverside California 92507
951-782-8050

Martin Fierro
Rocklin California 95677
916-630-0300

Phil Bluemel
Roseville California 95661
916-787-0555

Kim Fredrickson
Roseville California 95661
916-789-7082

Joan Buzzard
Sacramento California 95827
916-565-6307

Carol Lee
San Carlos California 94070
650-274-3140

Karen Lenell
San Diego California 92108
619-280-3430

G. Olson
San Diego California 92108
619-280-3430 ext. 122

Calvin Prather
San Diego California 92108
619-282-4600 ext. 2#

Donald Welch
San Diego California 92108
619-280-3430

Marilyn Lewis
San Diego California 92111
858-492-9985

Stephen Wilke
San Diego California 92127
858-592-0995

Clifford Stunden
San Dimas California 91773
626-367-9004

Sam Leong
San Francisco California 94114
415-550-6964

Matthew Lea
San Jose California 95124
408-881-0663

Mark Miller
San Jose California 95124
408-486-6763

Jonathon Arnold
San Mateo California 94404
650-570-7273

Connie Ratliffe
Santa Barbara California 93108
805-259-8949

Lee Langley
Santa Clarita California 91321
661-297-5728

Deborah Reed
Santa Clarita California 91355
661-287-4243

Ana-Margarita Sevcik
Santa Maria California 93454
805-619-0299

Vincent Staraci

Santa Monica California 90403
310-991-0553

Corrado Militi
Santa Monica California 90403
310-560-5112

Allison Hodge
Santa Monica California 90405
310-399-1617

Carolyn Dunn
Santa Rosa California 95403
707-571-1714 ext. 4

Cynthia Bohnker
Santa Rosa California 95404
707-364-7744

Stephen Morris
Santa Rosa California 95404
707-575-0550

Burton Walker
Santa Ynez California 93460
805-688-7779

Steven Brigham
Sherman Oaks California 91403
818-981-4071

Aleta Klein
Sierra Madre California 91024
626-795-2905

Robert Gross
Simi Valley California 93065
805-531-5160

Carol Thomsen
Sonora California 95370
209-536-9885

Cynthia Winn
South Pasadena California 91030
818-789-3346

Audrey Davidheiser
Studio City California 91604
818-985-1211

Sharilyn Johnson
Sun City California 92586
951-541-6216

John Lucas
Temecula California 92590
951-506-0662

Rick Shurtz
Thousand Oaks California 91361
805-529-8277

Laura Cavarretta
Thousand Oaks California 91361
805-497-7878

David Hoffman
Torrance California 90505
310-326-9654

Laurie Rotuna
Torrance California 90505
310-462-4285

Judy Alley
Torrance California 90505
310-791-6212

Douglas Hink
Tustin California 92780
714-544-8140

Kathy Lockridge
Tustin California 92780
714-669-9669

Robert Karman
Twentynine Palms California 92277
760-367-3290

Stephen Morris
Ukiah California 95482
707-575-0550

Kathryn Denham
Vacaville California 95688
707-447-4453

Susan Lee

Ventura California 93003
805-654-1422 ext. #4

David Wadman
Ventura California 93003
818-577-3015

Sandra Moe
Ventura California 93003
805-479-9980

Linda Montoya
Ventura California 93003
805-644-1650 ext. 420

Kris Mack
Ventura California 93003
805-644-1650 ext. 422

Donald Weintz
Visalia California 93277
559-738-0700

Arlys McDonald
Vista California 92084
760-727-6139

Elaine With
Walnut Creek California 94595
925-937-1245

Doris Dea
Walnut Creek California 94598
925-472-2556

Kami Leonard
West Hills California 91307-3936
818-754-2593

Allison Hodge
Westlake Village California 91361
805-497-6555

Teri Reisser
Westlake Village California 91361
805-370-1345

Kenji Watanabe
Westlake Village California 91362
818-266-3530

David Wadman
Westlake Village California 91362
818-577-3015

Luisa Segato Johnson
Westlake Vlg California 91362
818-707-6973

Philip Leidy
Whittier California 90601
562-696-3567

Philip Kaufman
Whittier California 90602
562-698-6737

Richard McMillan
Yorba Linda California 92886
714-558-9266 ext. 258

Robert Fromm
Yuba City California 95991
530-674-5296

Robert Karman
Yucca Valley California 92284
760-369-7167

Colorado

Barbara Russell
Aurora Colorado 80013
303-955-8851

Dane Russell
Aurora Colorado 80013
303-955-8851

Melissa Paulison
Aurora Colorado 80013
303-229-1080

Kevin Dyk
Aurora Colorado 80016
720-274-5272

Carol Hathaway-Clark

Boulder Colorado 80301
303-440-0295

Jay Lindsay
Boulder Colorado 80302
303-545-9828

Gary Johnson
Boulder Colorado 80303
720-545-4073

Jennifer Diebel
Boulder Colorado 80303
303-931-4284

Mary Murray
Broomfield Colorado 80020
720-933-7553

Joy Myers
Castle Rock Colorado 80108
303-643-8914

Catherine Daley
Castle Rock Colorado 80109
720-626-4299

William Myers
Centennial Colorado 80111
303-770-5999

Mark Humphries
Colorado Springs Colorado 80903
719-433-3034

Sam Jolman
Colorado Springs Colorado 80903
719-447-7446

Michael Bird
Colorado Springs Colorado 80907
719-219-3400

Marina Mayberry
Colorado Springs Colorado 80907
719-330-5554

Shari Edgell
Colorado Springs Colorado 80907
719-237-4799

Barbara Seeds
Colorado Springs Colorado 80907
719-633-4418

Marie Mortensen
Colorado Springs Colorado 80918
719-331-6754

Barry Ham
Colorado Springs Colorado 80918
719-495-5963

Charles Browning
Colorado Springs Colorado 80918
719-228-6560

Kay Harder
Colorado Springs Colorado 80918
719-548-8415

Glenn Lutjens
Colorado Springs Colorado 80918
719-359-3430

Geremy Keeton
Colorado Springs Colorado 80918
719-310-2995

Dale Schauer
Colorado Springs Colorado 80918
719-599-3080

Arnold Trillet
Colorado Springs Colorado 80920
719-337-2957

Betty Jordan
Colorado Springs Colorado 80923
719-510-8822

Paul Lam
Denver Colorado 80204
720-366-4635

Craig Loving
Denver Colorado 80209
303-349-7398

Andrew Jerusik

Englewood Colorado 80112
720-236-9624

Karin Steers
Estes Park Colorado 80517
720-252-6733

Renne Madison
Fort Collins Colorado 80524
970-324-6928

Chris Bassett
Fort Collins Colorado 80525
970-690-9350

David Donaldson
Golden Colorado 80401
303-643-8633

Susan Keortge-Cook
Golden Colorado 80401
303-205-8491

Saul Tompkins
Grand Junction Colorado 81501
970-241-2948

Stan Miller
Grand Junction Colorado 81501
970-241-2948

John Mason
Grand Junction Colorado 81506
970-245-3130

David Stewart
Greeley Colorado 80634
970-356-3081

Joy Myers
Greenwood Village Colorado 80111
303-643-8914

Craig Loving
Henderson Colorado 80640
303-349-7398

Mita Johnson
Lakewood Colorado 80215
303-808-8466

Adam Renfrow
Lakewood Colorado 80226
303-237-4680

C. Gilbert
Lakewood Colorado 80228
303-233-3338

Michele Santi
Lakewood Colorado 80401
303-506-0157

Kristin Hungerford
Littleton Colorado 80120
720-489-8555 ext. 104

Kirsten Christensen
Littleton Colorado 80120
303-997-0337

Katharine Cullis
Littleton Colorado 80120
303-810-2313

David Jenkins
Littleton Colorado 80120
303-730-1717

Susan Hein
Littleton Colorado 80121
303-921-2926

Grant Tschetter
Littleton Colorado 80127
303-201-1893

C. Gilbert
Lone Tree Colorado 80124
303-233-3338

Jay Lindsay
Longmont Colorado 80503
303-545-9828

Andrea Cartwright
Longmont Colorado 80503
720-352-2986

Jay Lindsay

Louisville Colorado 80027
303-545-9828

Michael Coen
Loveland Colorado 80538
970-217-2675

Carolyn Anna
Loveland Colorado 80538
970-222-9911

Steven Warner
Montrose Colorado 81401
970-252-1586

Craig Cato
Monument Colorado 80132
719-659-8423

Deborah Bauers Monument Colorado 80132
719-488-4673

Ron Veatch
Northglenn Colorado 80234
303-920-8771

John Mikitson
Northglenn Colorado 80234
720-217-2636

Dave Ragsdale
Parker Colorado 80134
303-324-6261

Craig Lounsbrough
Parker Colorado 80138
303-593-0575 ext. 123

Daniel Trathen
Parker Colorado 80138
303-593-0575

John Dengler
Pueblo West Colorado 81007
719-547-8300

Bruce Heany
Thornton Colorado 80229
303-212-2164

Renee Madison

Westminster Colorado 80031
303-257-7623

David Gutknecht
Westminster Colorado 80234
720-244-6418

Stacey Klein
Windsor Colorado 80550
970-222-3393

John West
Woodland Park Colorado 80866
719-290-8790

Connecticut

Charles Gardner
Greenwich Connecticut 06830
203-869-7269

Rafique Tai
Stamford Connecticut 06901
203-359-4624

Joseph DeAngelis
Sterling Connecticut 06377
401-439-4925

Florida

Norman Jaeger
Boca Raton Florida 33431
561-241-9014

Brent Gray
Boca Raton Florida 33431
561-241-9014 ext. 233

Martha Wibbels
Boca Raton Florida 33433
561-620-0089

Lily Corsello
Boca Raton Florida 33433
954-822-8874

Mary Ann Galle

Bradenton Florida 34209
941-795-7986

Marc Dillworth
Bradenton Florida 34210
941-755-8887

Sharon Otis
Bradenton Florida 34210
941-792-4988

John Lambert
Clearwater Florida 33756
727-492-4926

John Lambert
Clearwater Beach Florida 33767
727-492-4926

Alexander Gimon
Clermont Florida 34711
352-241-8540

Lilly Corsello
Fort Lauderdale Florida 33306
954-822-8874

Daniel Houmes
Fort Lauderdale Florida 33308
954-491-1314

Beverly Chestnut
Fort Myers Florida 33966
239-418-0369

Stephen Figley
Gainesville Florida 32607
352-380-0209

Linda Callahan
Gainesville Florida 32607
352-380-0209

C. Jefferson Hood
Jacksonville Florida 32216
904-725-1800

Stuart Whitlow
Jacksonville Florida 32223
904-262-1900

Stephanie Summers
Jacksonville Florida 32223
904-268-9178

Alice Fulghum
Jacksonville Florida 32257
904-762-4040

Brian Neal
Jupiter Florida 33458
561-427-3424

Alexander Gimon
Largo Florida 33771
727-584-1551

Cornelia Reynolds
Lutz Florida 33548
813-264-8771

Alan Alonso
Lutz Florida 33558
813-265-3859

Susan Cerni
Maitland Florida 32751
407-790-9149

Robert Bedworth
Melbourne Florida 32935
321-751-7000 ext. 24

Traci Jungkurth
Melbourne Florida 32940
321-253-8887

Bryan Myers
Merritt Island Florida 32953
321-480-1454

Kingsley Grant
Miami Florida 33168
786-236-3602

Larry Shyers
Mount Dora Florida 32757
352-383-2194

Dennis Cox

New Port Richey Florida 34652
727-849-0688

William Hicks
Orange Park Florida 32073
904-278-2717

Jan Amerman
Orlando Florida 32818
407-295-4381 ext 55

David Hatmaker
Orlando Florida 32819
407-704-1461

Kathryn Burckbuchler
Palm Beach Gardens Florida 33403
561-352-7022

Leslie Smith
Palm Beach Gardens Florida 33403
561-628-3916

Amy Oliver
Palm Beach Gardens Florida 33410
561-622-1771

Nathan Oliver
Palm Beach Gardens Florida 33410
561-622-1771

Kenneth Finch
Panama City Florida 32401
850-747-8144

Sandra Gilbert
Pensacola Florida 32534
850-505-7744

Grace Sidberry
Plantation Florida 33324
954-382-4889

Kevin Groeneveld
Pompano Beach Florida 33060
954-650-6348

James Fry
Port Charlotte Florida 33952
941-629-0440 ext. 3

Billie Burg
Seminole Florida 33772
727-392-1834

Tom Petit
St Petersburg Florida 33707
727-345-2318

John Goss
Tampa Florida 33612
813-935-3917

David Clarke
Tampa Florida 33614
813-879-4927

Robin Hanna
Vero Beach Florida 32967
772-559-6272

Georgia

Paul Cole
Athens Georgia 30606
706-552-0706

J. Loren James
Atlanta Georgia 30328
770-396-0232 ext. 227

Jim Ciraky
Canton Georgia 30115
404-293-5654

Bruce Atkinson
College Park Georgia 30349
770-439-9353

Carl Kissiah
Decatur Georgia 30033
770-938-1855

Stanley Hibbs
Dunwoody Georgia 30338
770-668-0350 ext. 224

Bruce Atkinson
Fayetteville Georgia 30214

770-439-9353

Walter Alton Jr.
Kennesaw Georgia 30144
770-262-2743

Yolanda Monteiro
Lawrenceville Georgia 30044
770-806-0082

Jim Ciraky
Marietta Georgia 30064
404-293-5654

Bob Grant
Marietta Georgia 30067
404-579-4437

Penny Harger
Norcross Georgia 30071
770-246-0467

William Baughman
Powder Springs Georgia 30127
770-222-1980

Dee-Sharon Goar
Roswell Georgia 30075
770-992-4956

J. Loren James
Roswell Georgia 30076
770-797-6723

Tim Bouman
Roswell Georgia 30076
404-271-9009

Keith Niager
Savannah Georgia 31406
912-352-7638

Arthur Hartzell
Savannah Georgia 31406
912-354-7607

Jim Ciraky
Smyrna Georgia 30082
404-293-5654

Rich Lewis

Stockbridge Georgia 30281
770-474-8400

Jim Ciraky
Stockbridge Georgia 30281
404-293-5654

Tracy Limes
Woodstock Georgia 30189
770-605-9543

Hawaii

Hale Akamine
Honolulu Hawaii 96814
808-592-2500

Idaho

Terry Pape
Boise Idaho 83705
208-343-0441

Janice Stramel
Fruitland Idaho 83619
208-452-4378

John Oakley
Idaho Falls Idaho 83404
208-522-1222

Jeff Eastman
Twin Falls Idaho 83303
208-841-4837

Illinois

Edward Senkpeil
Barrington Illinois 60010
847-651-8489

Karen Lindenmeyer
Bolingbrook Illinois 60440
630-632-1653

James Natter
Carol Stream Illinois 60188
630-752-9750

Dale Petre
Champaign Illinois 61821
217-359-0559

James Klein
Champaign Illinois 61822
217-363-1700

Eva Ponder
Chicago Illinois 60610
312-573-8864

Abayomi Nichols
Chicago Illinois 60615
815-944-8844

John Sample
Cordova Illinois 61242
309-654-2402

Joyce Stewart
Edwardsville Illinois 62025-3890
618-210-3500

Larry Quicksall
Effingham Illinois 62401
217-347-5937

Shirley Burnside
Elmhurst Illinois 60126
630-941-9123

Janet Voss
Evanston Illinois 60201
847-764-9231

Thomas Suk
Evanston Illinois 60201
847-492-1938

Dennis Gibson
Glen Ellyn Illinois 60137
630-668-3331

Edward Senkpeil
Grayslake Illinois 60030

847-651-8489

Deborah McFadden
Hanover Park Illinois 60133
630-372-6599

David McFadden
Hanover Park Illinois 60133
630-372-6599

David Mackinnon
Hinsdale Illinois 60521
630-325-4770

Pamela Rak
Hoffman Estates Illinois 60169
847-776-1594

Larry Simcox
Joliet Illinois 60431
630-653-5405

Robert Laib
Joliet Illinois 60433
815-725-5188

Janet Voss
Lake Bluff Illinois 60044
847-764-9231

Clark Barshinger
Lake Zurich Illinois 60047
847-438-4222

Allan Peterson
Lyons Illinois 60534
708-308-4141

John Sample
Moline Illinois 61265
309-757-7141

Stephen Wissel
Mount Carmel Illinois 62863
618-263-2707

Janet Voss
Northfield Illinois 60093
847-764-9231

James Quandt
Oak Park Illinois 60304
708-445-9330

Larry Simcox
Oswego Illinois 60543
630-653-5405

Edward Senkpeil
Palatine Illinois 60067
847-651-8489

Martin Stuck
Palatine Illinois 60067
847-593-6774

Ronald Martinez
Rock Island Illinois 61201
309-793-5000

Shari Ramsey
Rockford Illinois 61107
815-988-4163

James Parrish
Rockford Illinois 61108
815-229-7102

Robert Laib
Shorewood Illinois 60404
815-725-5188

David McFadden
South Elgin Illinois 60177
847-488-1999

Deborah McFadden
South Elgin Illinois 60177
847-488-1999

Susan Yarrington
Springfield Illinois 62711
217-698-7150

George Cook
Urbana Illinois 61801
217-239-0142

Edward Mchugh
Western Springs Illinois 60558

708-246-8695

Christine Davis
Wheaton Illinois 60187
630-653-1717

Larry Simcox
Wheaton Illinois 60187
630-653-5405

Karen Watson-Jarvis
Wheaton Illinois 60187
630-653-1717

William Rhodes
Zion Illinois 60099
847-731-3192

Indiana

Donna Ganote
Brownsburg Indiana 46112
317-848-5600

Donna Ganote
Carmel Indiana 46032
317-848-5600

Vickie Knowlden
Evansville Indiana 47710
812-483-2364

Andrew Hatfield
Evansville Indiana 47712
812-319-5810

Paul McDaniel
Fishers Indiana 46038
317-578-9200

Heidi Easterly
Fort Wayne Indiana 46815
260-485-4357

Todd Yoder
Fort Wayne Indiana 46815
260-485-4357

Dereck Paris
Fort Wayne Indiana 46815
260-485-4357

Wayne Von Bargen
Fort Wayne Indiana 46825
260-471-8033

Alfred Barrow
Greenwood Indiana 46143
317-888-0581

Connie Tooley
Greenwood Indiana 46143
317-888-0581

Michael O'Brien
Indianapolis Indiana 46203
317-797-2767

Boyce Ruegsegger
Indianapolis Indiana 46254
317-293-5563

Jennifer Wheat
Indianapolis Indiana 46256
317-585-1060 ext. 23

Robert Muller
Kendallville Indiana 46755
260-343-0908

Shawn Pogue
Seymour Indiana 47274
812-523-0386 ext. 101

John Thompson
Terre Haute Indiana 47803
812-232-2144

David Bauer
Valparaiso Indiana 46383
219-477-5646

Jennifer Wheat
Whitestown Indiana 46075
317-585-1060 ext. 23

Gary Vaughn
Yorktown Indiana 47396

765-288-6266

Iowa

Marty Martinez
Ames Iowa 50010
515-460-6360

Marty Martinez
Ames Iowa 50014
515-294-0168

Lonnie Marshall
Cedar Rapids Iowa 52402
319-393-6796

Colleen Hunter
Cedar Rapids Iowa 52402
319-377-2161

Lonnie Marshall
Coralville Iowa 52241
1-800-467-3165

Matthew Burch
Pella Iowa 50219
641-628-1723

Donald Gilbert
West Des Moines Iowa 50266
515-225-4006

Kansas

Stan Seymour
El Dorado Kansas 67042
316-321-2878

Annette Stanley
Leawood Kansas 66224
913-626-9915

Judson Swihart
Manhattan Kansas 66502
785-776-4105

Dennis Smith
Olathe Kansas 66062

913-530-4736

Michael Priddy
Overland Park Kansas 66216
913-449-3696

Troy Reiner
Wichita Kansas 67204
316-838-9200

Donna Botinelly
Wichita Kansas 67205
316-722-2848

Angela Bogue-Gilmore
Wichita Kansas 67206
316-631-1280

Alyssa Donnelly
Wichita Kansas 67206
316-866-2800

Randy Storms
Wichita Kansas 67208
316-260-2525

Philip Ashley
Wichita Kansas 67226
316-683-4083

Lee Ellen Patterson
Wichita Kansas 67226
316-683-4083

Aaron Scharenberg
Wichita Kansas 67226
316-683-4083

Kentucky

Diana Caillouet
Bowling Green Kentucky 42104
270-782-6121

Richard Meyer
Florence Kentucky 41042
859-371-2800

Mikki Taylor
Henderson Kentucky 42420
270-826-4952

Jane Hill
Henderson Kentucky 42420
270-826-8761

Marydora Conley
Jeffersontown Kentucky 40299
502-500-1553

James Ross
Lexington Kentucky 40502
859-278-3290

Dan Pugel
Lexington Kentucky 40504
859-514-6061

Paul Schmidt
Lexington Kentucky 40508
502-633-2860

James Kassel
Louisville Kentucky 40223
502-339-4511

Joseph Arnold
Louisville Kentucky 40241
502-384-2844

Paul Schmidt
Louisville Kentucky 40243
502-244-4407

Joseph Williams
Mayfield Kentucky 42066
270-247-5667

Wanda Staley
Mount Sterling Kentucky 40353
859-498-5953

Stephen Johnson
Nicholasville Kentucky 40356
859-219-9800

Roger Thompson
Paducah Kentucky 42001

270-442-5738

Paul Schmidt
Shelbyville Kentucky 40065
502-633-2860

James Rayburn
Versailles Kentucky 40383
859-879-9406

Louisiana

Rogers Butner
Baton Rouge Louisiana 70802
225-387-2287

Vicky Benton
Baton Rouge Louisiana 70816
225-273-0106

Dickie Walden
Bossier City Louisiana 71112
318-746-5600

Todd Capielano
Jefferson Louisiana 70121
504-734-0501

Marc D'Aunoy
Lafayette Louisiana 70503
337-889-0221

Cynthia Shrewsberry
Lake Charles Louisiana 70601
337-478-1616

Maine

Paul Gervais
Augusta Maine 04330
207-622-0713

E. Dennis Marasco
Bangor Maine 04401
207-973-6199

Jane Marasco
Bangor Maine 04401

207-973-6199

Maryland

Martha Herb
Annapolis Maryland 21401
410-266-8345

William Williams
Annapolis Maryland 21401
410-266-8345

Elizabeth Krakow
Annapolis Maryland 21401
410-266-8345

David Ochinero
Arnold Maryland 21012
410-975-0105

Patricia Gaffney
Ellicott City Maryland 21042
410-782-0048

Doris Morgan
Ellicott City Maryland 21043
410-750-3330

Jane Harman
Frederick Maryland 21702
301-662-8900

Carol Ambrose
Hancock Maryland 21750
301-667-6327

Doris Morgan
Lutherville-Timonium Maryland 21093
410-561-9584

Helen McDowell
Rockville Maryland 20850
301-315-9009

Carol Ambrose
Rockville Maryland 20850
301-667-6327

Massachusetts

Cynthia Fisher
Beverly Massachusetts 01915
978-524-4889

Vinnie Cappetta
Hopkinton Massachusetts 1748
508-293-1611

Samuel Schutz
Ipswich Massachusetts 01938
978-406-1321

Chalres Slagen
Lexington Massachusetts 02421
781-402-2442

Charles Slagen
Marlborough Massachusetts 01752
508-787-1048

Michigan

Gregory Hocott
Ann Arbor Michigan 48108
734-477-9999

Karen Theisen
Battle Creek Michigan 49015
269-979-8119

Thomas Shelder
Cadillac Michigan 49601
231-645-3735

Luke Stephan
Canton Michigan 48187
734-737-1200 ext. 1180

Daphne DeMaris
Clarkston Michigan 48346
586-202-0474

Dorothy Siegl
Dearborn Michigan 48124
313-274-4570

Victoria Coyne
Detroit Michigan 48236
313-343-9000

Janet Wiles
Flint Michigan 48507
810-235-2500

Jesse Soulia
Flint Michigan 48532
810-732-6111

Samuel Roth
Grand Rapids Michigan 49506
616-831-2000

Dave Vander Wal
Grand Rapids Michigan 49508
616-457-2277

Ken Adams
Grand Rapids Michigan 49512
616-949-9550

Jan Bentley
Grand Rapids Michigan 49512
616-949-9550

Allen Hoogewind
Grand Rapids Michigan 49546
616-942-7331

David Burke
Grandville Michigan 49418
616-485-9167

Daphne DeMaris
Grosse Pointe Michigan 48230
586-202-0474

Kathryn Salmi
Hancock Michigan 49930
906-482-2231

Chris Augustine
Kalamazoo Michigan 49008
269-345-0909

Barry Brigham

Kalamazoo Michigan 49009
269-375-4363

Andrew Wichterman
Kalamazoo Michigan 49009
269-375-4363

James Dignan
Livonia Michigan 48154
734-788-0842

A. Todd Henderson
Northville Michigan 48167
734-756-3815

Jack Woodburn
Port Huron Michigan 48060
810-984-5575

Daniel Austin
Rochester Hills Michigan 48306
248-496-1088

Sam Cherian
Royal Oaks Michigan 48067
2486773901

Renee Williams
Southfield Michigan 48076
248-557-8390

Debra Cargo
Spring Lake Michigan 49456
616-844-0507

Marcia Wiinamaki
Stevensville Michigan 49127
269-429-7727

Thomas Shelder
Traverse City Michigan 49684
231-645-3735

Janice Acker
Trenton Michigan 48183
734-675-9700

Kathy Barton
Troy Michigan 48083
586-419-2377

Marion Turowski
Troy Michigan 48084
248-269-8730

Minnesota

Steven Erickson
Apple Valley Minnesota 55124
952-432-3220

Brent Baumler
Burnsville Minnesota 55337
952-892-8495

Sheila Marker
Burnsville Minnesota 55337
952-892-8495

Cynthia Gill
Chanhassen Minnesota 55317
952-974-3999

Marshall Fightlin
Duluth Minnesota 55802
218-722-4379

Gary Vikesland
Golden Valley Minnesota 55427
763-525-8590

Irene Burbul
Inver Grove Heights Minnesota 55077
351-230-6140

Tim Johnson
Lake Elmo Minnesota 55042
651-379-0444

Timothy Wiertzema
Lake Elmo Minnesota 55042
651-379-0444

Anita Smith
Mankato Minnesota 56001
800-438-1772

Ying Pang Elliot
Minneapolis Minnesota 55427

763-525-8590 ext. 290

Peg Roberts
Minnetonka Minnesota 55305
952-546-5565

William Rush
Minnetonka Minnesota 55305
952-546-4044

Carol Brown
Minnetonka Minnesota 55305
952-546-4044

Daniel Loe
New Ulm Minnesota 56073
507-354-1147

John McKenzie
Rochester Minnesota 55901
507-529-7625

Terry Riley
ROCHESTER Minnesota 55906
507-254-3380

Loren Hubin
Saint Paul Minnesota 55112
651-482-9361

William Rush
Stillwater Minnesota 55082
651-439-2059

Mississippi

Barbara Martin
Jackson Mississippi 39209
601-923-1635

Elizabeth Burton
Oxford Mississippi 38655
662-259-7211

Steve Roark
Yazoo City Mississippi 39194
662-571-7803

Michael Miller

Ballwin Missouri 63011
636-394-5553

Linda Teague
Bowling Green Missouri 63334
636-734-5170

Ryan Pannell
Branson Missouri 65616
417-336-5652

Paul Wang
Chesterfield Missouri 63017
314-721-7777

David Bailey
Chesterfield Missouri 63017
314-954-5779

Linda Hermann
Clayton Missouri 63105
314-504-6015

Edna Mae Farmer
Columbia Missouri 65240
543-499-4572

Keith White
Grandview Missouri 64030
816-765-8211

Linda Smith
Higginsville Missouri 64037
816-456-6654

Christopher Cornine
Independence Missouri 64057
816-373-9240 ext. 301

Jill Lillard
Jefferson City Missouri 65109-5861
800-797-0191

Cheryl Costabil
Kansas City Missouri 64147
816-985-0336

Barry McAnulty
Lees Summit Missouri 64063
816-554-0912

Hal Pendergrass
Maryland Heights Missouri 63043
314-298-0900

Janell McIntyre
Nixa Missouri 65714
417-848-5574

Judy Koehler
Saint Louis Missouri 63105
314-249-5444

Linda Bryan
Saint Louis Missouri 63122
314-560-4622

Sue McClure
Saint Louis Missouri 63122
314-750-1850

Tai Yong
Saint Louis Missouri 63132
314-496-3922

William Kuntz
Saint Louis Missouri 63139
314-712-1754

Harold Bloss
Saint Louis Missouri 63141
636-230-4756

Julia Reid
Saint Louis Missouri 63141
314-469-5522 ext. 15

Judy Schmidt
Saint Louis Missouri 63146
314-569-4114

James Harris III
Springfield Missouri 65804
417-224-3358

Cindy Irwin
Springfield Missouri 65804
417-827-6245

Montana

Robert Bakko
Billings Montana 59101
406-259-6161

Sharon Nason
Helena Montana 59601
406-443-8580

Kathleen Bradford
Missoula Montana 59801
406-532-1574

Jim Ramsey
Missoula Montana 59803
406-251-7073

Oklahoma

Jason Gunter
Oklahoma City Oklahoma 73120
405-752-9500

Pennsylvania

David Rogers
Hershey Pennsylvania 17033
717-533-5311

South Carolina

Robert Smith
Hilton Head Island South Carolina 29928
843-785-4099

John McLain
Lyman South Carolina 29365-1761
864-706-6383

Tennessee

Don Harvey
Brentwood Tennessee 37027
615-376-4818

Nathan Jernigan
Murfreesboro Tennessee 37129
615-896-1305

Texas

Meredith Akin
Arlington Heights Texas 76013-3407
817-723-1210

Peter Bradley
Flower Mound Texas 75028
469-635-7540

Melinda Goudeau
Richardson Texas 75080
972-437-4698

Virginia

Brenda Lundie
South Chesterfield Virginia 23834
804-526-0424

A bride, a wife

Toni Henderson-Mayers is a sought after speaker whose message encourages us all to build better personal and business relationships. Her book, Wise Courtship, originally published in 2013 went worldwide and has impacted many lives.

She is the co-author of the book, "One Great Idea" and a contributing writer to the book "Share and Grow Rich" both available on her website.

Toni lives in North Carolina with her husband and two sons writing, travelling, speaking and performing throughout the country. Learn more about Toni Henderson-Mayers at www.WiseCourtship.com.

More Love Gifts

Life Coaches help you to accomplish personal achievements or professional success. Contact Toni for a free 15 minute premarital or life coaching session.

Toni Henderson-Mayers
www.WiseCourtship.com
info@WiseCourtship.com

Upcoming Books

Wise Courtship: Q & A
Wise Courtship: See it. Believe it.
Wise Courtship: Dig Deeper
Wise Courtship: Revelation

Purchase Toni's book, "One Great Idea". Order by visiting her website: www.WiseCourtship.com

What people are saying about Wise Courtship

This is a well thought out work that provides important spiritual guidance for couples to move towards marital success in a secular world of frequent marriage dissolutions and painful impact on children. This author is truly on point. Read it now!

> **-Sharon W. Cooper, MD FAAP**
> **Developmental and Forensic Pediatrician**
> **University of North Carolina at Chapel Hill School of Medicine**

From the moment I started reading Wise Courtship, I knew we needed to have Toni on the show because she had a powerful message to share. Her book transforms how you think about dating and equips you with a how-to guide for choosing the right mate for you.

During her interview she was thought-provoking and engaging, and left our viewers wanting more!

As a single woman, I've subscribed to the Wise Courtship Philosophy. I'm now an avid follower of Toni because her words of wisdom are just what I've needed in my quest for love.

-Joy Sutton, TV Host/Executive Producer, *Joy Sutton Show*

Wise Courtship is a must read for anyone seeking proper preparation for healthy relationships. Toni tackles the relationship topics that are frequently overlooked, but necessary for long-lasting and happy relationships.

-Yolanda, Minnesota

Toni Henderson-Mayers is truly a master at what she does. I have watched her broadcast both live and replays, they are a representation of her book, Wise Courtship. She is very knowledgeable in her area of expertise and clear in delivery. As a married woman, I find her words of wisdom for not only singles but also those who are married. I certainly recommend her book any day.

-Dr. Princess Fumi Hancock, DNP, MA, BSN
Bestselling Author, African Oscar Winning Filmmaker, & Publishing Strategist

I just wanted to send you a quick email, saying thank you for all of your scopes that you do every day. I watch your replays every night before I go to bed, and, I was so happy to have caught you live this morning to let you know that I had purchased your book, and that I had just received it in the mail a few days ago. Your scopes have really helped me since I have struggled with relationships (love, friendships, and business!! All the above!!) for so long now. Many of my numerous broken relationships in the past have really taken an emotional toll on me for so many years. Some of which I still haven't gotten over after many years have past. I am really happy to have your scopes and your book now to help me, and guide me with my current and future relationships. And to even help me cope with understanding my past relationships that were fractured for reasons that were out of my control.

Thank you again for your scopes, and I am looking forward to spending more time reading Wise Courtship during my Thanksgiving break.

Take care,

-Jason, San Francisco Bay, California

Jason's Follow up after reading Wise Courtship….

I'm so happy that I bought the book. I know this will help me with my future relationships. I especially found the real life cases in the book to be very informative. This is definitely a must read for anyone who is seeking help with his/her relationships.

    -Jason, San Francisco Bay, California

Toni is best at giving relationship advice without fluff. That's why I always invite her back on my show, Gfem Talk Show.

    -Femi "Gfem" Ogunjinmi, author of Revelations of Relationship

After reading Wise Courtship...I think what it did for us was to slow us down and come to the realization that we have a lot of work to do before we could even consider marriage. Although we love each other and have a long history; two children and four grandchildren together. We don't seem to have what it takes to be in a healthy relationship. He's most definitely not romantic and he barely pay's me a complement. What he does is pay the bills, cooks and he's a great handyman, but that's not enough. I want him to cherish the ground that I walk on. I believe that we've allowed outside influences to cause the breakdown in our relationship. We call the outsiders "FAMILY." We find ourselves spending more time trying to get everyone else's lives together and what we've done is neglect our own lives. What we've discovered by reading your book together is that we have to refocus our attention on each other and not allow others to cause potential conflict because we decided that we do not want to become any of those case studies that you talked about in your book. Lol. The good news is that we're mature enough to know what we want and how to go about achieving it. Next Tuesday, Jan. 26th we will begin our marriage counseling sessions and we truly look forward to it because help is so needed at this point.

-Robin, NJ

Honestly I really don't know where or how to start but all I know for sure is that Toni Henderson-Mayers is one of the ladies I admire so much both on and off the Periscope community. Ms. Henderson-Mayers determination to equip people with tools to create flourishing relationships is clearly seen in her daily scopes on Periscope. Each day her selflessness, hard work and tenacity plays out right in front of us as she continues to provide scopes that is aimed at helping us have better relationships both in our personal and organizations lives.

I can't forget the major role she played in helping me understand how to make lasting relationship choices, and I do know for sure that many other people can testify to this as well. I enjoy watching Ms. Toni's s daily scopes on Periscope.tv because it is always uplifting, inspiring, informative and educative, and has just the right ingredients that will help individuals like me and you build sustainable healthy relationships.

Thank you Toni Henderson-Mayes for your determination to help humanity have a better relationship through this powerful book, WISE COURTSHIP.

God bless you!

-Nkechi Ajaeroh, Williamsburg, VA, Blogger at Peristart.com & Founder Afriscope Periscope

Toni is an engaging and knowledgeable teacher/trainer. Her lessons on Wise Courtships are solid and based on sound wisdom and practical experience. It is clear as she teaches that she is passionate about her topic and that her motivation is to see people create and develop relationships that are strong, lasting, healthy and fulfilling. She teaches foundational principles and offers practical advice that can take you from confusion and wonder to knowledge and power. If you haven't had the opportunity to hear her share her wisdom, I highly recommend that you check her out.

    -Vita Panico Vice-President - Green Galaxy Companies Inc. Toronto, ON Canada

Excellent read. The counsel is on point, and very relevant to modern relationships. Even though I am married, it had me thinking, "Darn, where was this BEFORE I got married?"

    -Elder Tirell A. M. Clifton I, MDiv, Maryland

Toni Henderson-Mayers book, Wise Courtship is a must read for everyone. Toni tells the real truth; GOD's truth about courting.

    -Mary Smith-Moore, Radio Host, Christians Destined to Reign

The WISE COURTSHIP Philosophy is golden.

Toni Henderson-Mayers gives the tools that help identify REAL-ationships and proper marriage preparation.

Toni teaches the lost art of courtship and shows that it is the best time to deal with and/or avoid the issues that often catch couples by surprise AFTER the wedding.

These principles can help couples start strong and are continuously applicable, even many years after leaving the altar, for maintaining healthy marriages.

-LeRoy A. Smith, New Jersey

Toni Henderson- Mayers' book "Wise Courtship" is a much needed companion for single women everywhere. Thank you Toni for sharing the word!

-Sonya Evans Oates, NC

I am moved by the inspiration through her broadcasts and written words. I have been trying in the past to develop better relationships but when I heard the inspiration through Ms. Toni's broadcast, I kept telling myself, you can do this. You deserve peace and happiness. It made me question my overall life. I am always on the lookout for the next book or product because it is blessing my life.

-Ericka Rush, Tallahassee, FL

Wise Courtship is awesome. I promote it 100%.

-Keith L. Wagner, Texas

The Wise Courtship book is a practical book that will help you improve your marital relationships. This book is long overdue and greatly needed.

-Dr. Reginald A. Wells, Pastor, Falling Run Missionary Baptist Church, Fayetteville, North Carolina

I learned about the wise courtship philosophy back when you had your book launch. I wasn't able to attend but I did purchase your book on kindle. Great advice, I'm definitely applying some of it now and going forward in my relationships.

-Pamila Robinson, NJ

LaTanya Rice

Celebrity Hair Braider
Toni's Personal Stylist
(910) 273-4389